A Jar of Sticklebacks

A Jar of Sticklebacks
First eBook edition published October 2011
This POD edition first published in October 2013
by Armadillo Central Limited
Great Britain

Photographs: © Sylvia Selzer
Cover Artwork: Jennifer Copley-May
Cover Design: Daz Smith/Jennifer Copley-May
Book Design: Caroline Reeves

© Armadillo Central 2011

POD ISBN: 978-1-908539-15-1
Armadillo Central Limited
PO Box 897, Richmond, Surrey, TW9 9EH, UK

www.armadillocentral.com

A Jar of Sticklebacks

David Selzer

ARMADILLO
CENTRAL

For Evie

Contents

A Short History

For a generation, like weather cocks,
their skeletons swung near the highway.
James Price and Thomas Brown had robbed the Mail.
Years turned. The Gowy flooded and the heath
flowered. Travellers noted the bones
hanging in chains by the Warrington road.
Justices ordered the gibbet removed,
the remains disposed of. In Price's skull,
while Napoleon was crossing the Alps
or Telford building bridges or Hegel
defining Historical Necessity
or Goya painting Wellington's portrait,
a robin made its nest.

Portrait of the Artist

The hard back quarto exercise book opens
at 'A New Valentine', an unfinished,
blank verse piece – full of Auden, Larkin, Yeats –
in thick nib fountain pen on feint ruled lines.
Four decades old and more – and pristine:
'Today, at best, brings scented, satin hearts,
Numb messengers of somebody's desires...'

I can see the back room in the shared flat:
sagging bed, faded armchair, torn carpet,
wobbly table; I'd brought a large ashtray,
a glass fronted bookcase and a small, handmade
Chinese cabinet. A tv blared upstairs.
Through the sash window stuck fast with paint
was the littered garden – out of sight and
sound, all of Liverpool, swinging city.

The cabinet – carved drawers filled now with years
of love – was a woman's gift to a man
coming of age. (But I was still a boy
then full of needs and fears and words).
Borne on the leafy fretwork of the doors,
two gilded, lacquered kingfishers in flight,
sun catching on their iridescent wings,
fall together into oblivion.

At Mycenae 1984

Behind the lintel of the Lion Gate,
swallows had built their nest. Two Mirage jets,
burning Nato dollars, buzzed the valley.
A sweat-stained, overweight American
squatted in the shade of the ashlar ramparts,
fanning himself with a bush hat. "Hey, which
pile of stones is this?" A veteran's pension
kept him in exile. His mom and dad
had once stood arm-in-arm with that eager,
cropped marine recruit, who was altogether now
someone else. Thanksgiving and each birthday,
he would call collect. "This is the country
to screw up with your folks!"… He lies in the bunker,
smoking a joint. The black sergeant plays Hendrix
on his new Hitachi. From six miles
up the valley, NVA artillery
blow their minds... Parts of his skull were wired
like a broken vase. On the tourist bus,
his compatriots avoided him.
He smelt of despair, was a friend, a son,
brother missing in firefields of tattered
flags. Survivor's guilt confounds. How he longed
to talk of Khe Sanh, how often spoke of
America! Swallows dipped above him,
under the gate. He did not look at them.

Far Above Rubies

The silence woke her. Beyond the locked door
by now her maids should be chattering
in that harsh tongue. She went to the window.
Even the gulls on the battlements were mute.
And no guards on the ramparts, nobody
in the bailey. The straits were the colour
of the emerald at her neck – her father's
wedding gift. A barque moved edgily
through the sands. Its pennants spoke of home.
The island's coast was clear in the sun.
She imagined the light summer wind
stirring its fecund, strategic fields.

Her door was unlocked, opened and flung wide.
The Prince held a red cloth. "Cover your eyes."
As she tied the cloth in place, he said,
"Who can find a virtuous woman?"
He put his hand in the small of her back,
steering her from her chamber into his,
impelling her to the window. She felt
the gentle air from the valley, inhaled
the woods and the river. He pulled the cloth
hard from her head. Eyes shocked wide in death,
her lover hung from a gibbet. She watched
the body move this way, that way; listened
to the rope creak; turned to her husband.
"Until I die, I shall count the years
I will have loved him as a benison."

Looking for Puffins:
South Stack Revisited –
A Poem for Our Daughter

'South Stack Ynys Môn', 2009

Of course, by the time it's my turn at the 'scope
the bugger's turned its back. 'It is a puffin,'
reassures the RSPB girl – and,
since she's pretty and young, I believe
that what I see is not one of the teeming,
noisy, noisome, nesting guillemots,
razorbills or gulls. A hat trick: ageism,
sexism, anthropomorphism – plus
being *churlish as a bear* rather than
valiant as a lion. Intriguing opposites. Grrr!

We came here last when she was five or six.
Decades on, she stands with her lover
at a turn in the steps – both happy,
both blooming with her longed-for future,
and wrestling with the breeze for your camera.

Some gulls have eschewed the crowded cliffs to nest
in the lighthouse's disused kitchen garden.
We lean on the wall like pig farmers.
There is a dead chick amongst the gooseberries.
A living one stands, yes, surprised, startled but
resolute though even here winds roar like lions
or bears. I hold my breath…1,2,3…
for us all.

The Valley of the Amarici, Kwazulu Natal,

April 2006

'Window, Ancestors' House – Kwazulu-Natal', 2006

Elijah is our guide, Michael our mentor –
Mandla and Mbuzeni – old enough
to have needed 'white' names.

"They are not tourists", Mbuzeni explains,
as we meet healers, dancers, wedding guests.
He is politely disbelieved.
The expensive camera appears to betray us.
"They are big people," begins Mandla –
an old woman interrupts, speaking to me:
"Hey, Mister Man, what do you want?"
I explain, try to reassure. "I have worked
in the gold mines, Mister Man. I know you."

Legend has it renegades from Shaka Zulu
hid in the valley, became cannibal.
In the not so long ago past,
male children had their cheeks scored,
as infants, to drain the bad blood.
Mandla stops a friend on horseback,
who willingly shows us the three
horizontal scars on each cheek.

We stay at Mbuzeni's house. Through the night
there is distant drumming. We wake early
to a loudspeaker moving through the valley,
electioneering. This is Inkhata country.

We can see from his house a thick belt of alien
poplar trees far beyond the high grass
at the foot of a slope – a screen for an alpine-type resort.
We eat there – Mbuzeni, Mandla, the only black guests.
A friend and neighbour from the valley serves us.
The other guests stare. We become angry.
"What is now law is not yet lore!" says Mandla, laughing.
"We are where we are, guys," says Mbuzeni, softly.

Accidents

A sudden heavy shower of summer rain
slows the early evening motorway
to a blood red blur of brake lights.
In my mirror, I see two cars collide,
career across the lanes – and others stop,
receding out of sight into the downpour…

I am thirteen and a half and tall for my age –
the year of Hungary and Suez;
am sitting on the red leather back seat
of an almost straight-from-the-showroom
Morris Minor (in the inexorable green),
having dined at Heathrow's new, five star
restaurant and sampled *hors d'oeuvre*
and tasted *Riesling* for the first time;
am being driven back to Golders Green
by Yvette, the car's owner, a fashion designer
and childhood friend of the other passenger,
Angela, my aunt, a night club pianist,
briefly home from Johannesburg –
both daughters of Tzarist refugees,
both light years from the Pale,
bleached blondes, smoking Sobranie
Black Russian in ivory cigarette holders;
am listening to these nubile women,

our daughter's age now, talk acidly
of their exes, wearily of their dads
when a four door car, overtaking,
somewhere on the Great West Road,
comes seemingly too close and Yvette
swerves sharply right, her bumper
striking its fender with a metallic thump...

Fifty and more years later I forget
the dénouement. Certainly, no one died.
I think of you, somewhere perhaps without rain,
watching the sun set, perhaps wondering where I am,
why I am late, while I drive homewards.

Under November Skies

The rain has stopped. We can hear only the wind
and a swollen stream – hidden beneath
the high moor's golden fern – rush through a culvert
under the road, which glistens, after the shower,
in an unexpected shaft of sunlight.
Rain clouds are blackening the mountains
to the west but northwards, beyond bracken
and gorse that stretches seemingly to land's edge,
through a gap in the hills, we can see the sea,
a sunny blue, and a white ship sailing east –
too far away to recognise her flags.
Chance has brought us here as winter comes. Love
stays us against the dark.

Chuzpah

A nor' easterly blew – over Dutchman Bank –
on the front at Beaumaris, so we had
our chips, fish and mushy peas in the Vectra,
watching the ebb tide slowly, slowly expose
the furrowed gold of the Lavin Sands
and the cormorants and oyster catchers
skim the waves, when, suddenly, a herring gull,
that voracious omnivore, that frequenter
of rubbish tips and landfills, landed on our
bonnet and, not six feet from a town council
notice forbidding the feeding of said beasts,
watched us eat each pea, chip, fish flake and morsel
of batter (meanwhile blocking the view) and then
just buggered off – the colours of its plumage,
eyes and skin pristine, as if painted.

George Gershwin at
Chirk Castle

As we walk up the steep driveway, stopping
for breath at the curve where the castle
comes into sight – raised to block the routes
through the Dee Valley and Glyn Ceiriog
to starve the Welsh – a beribboned Rolls
descends, bride waving, followed, on foot,
by the wedding party in straggles –
black suits and brown shoes, wispy wedding hats –
treading the incline with tipsy effort.

George Gershwin, born Jacob Gershovitz,
the second son of Russian immigrants,
ex song plugger in Tin Pan Alley
at Remick's on West 28th Street,
in his thirtieth year visits Europe,
renews acquaintance with Alban Berg,
Ravel, Poulenc, Milhaud, Prokofiev
and William Walton, hears *Rhapsody in Blue*
and *Concerto in F* performed in Paris.

From the grassed walk above the Ha-ha,
we can see the main gates, unused now,
the lane to the station, the Cadbury
and MDF factories, the market town
of Chirk itself and, beyond, the panorama –
from Bickerton Hills to The Long Mynd –
as we follow the trail of illicit confetti
to the Doric Temple aka summerhouse.

The 8th Lord Howard De Walden – Tommy
to friends and family, Eton and Sandhurst,
Boer War and Great War, race horse owner,
playwright, theatre impresario –
turned its 14th century chapel
into a concert hall and invited George.

The westering sun shines upon us, dreaming
in the Temple, your head upon my shoulder.
A flock of starlings swarms suddenly
above the town – waltzing, deceiving like
a net, substantial, delicate – and is gone.

There is no public record of what he played
or when or how he got here. I like to think
he chose the stopping train from Paddington,

to work on *An American in Paris*,
and that Tommy met him personally
at Chirk Station, drove him up the hill,
in his Hispano-Suiza, through the baroque
wrought iron gates replete with wolves' and eagles' heads –
and as they, genius and renaissance man,
chatted about the history of the place,
along the chestnut lined drive among
the grazing sheep, George thought of Brooklyn's
geometric streets and of Manhattan's roar.

Lost

After the fluorescent shops and the snatched music,
the side street was damp and dark –
but a bag of chips and a manipulative adult
made the emptiness freedom.

Waterways were trawled and the usual,
time-dishonoured suspects questioned.
Down river, high tides returned her nine year old body.

The funeral cortège was a carriage and horses
and the local press was effulgent.
But gossip condemned her single mother,
living in a hostel on benefit.

The killer lived two floors down,
an estranged father of daughters –
a violent drunk, unemployed, unschooled.

Victim, mother and murderer
threaten the equivocal city.
Losers and losing
challenge its achievements.

Death is only one result of murder.
Remember sweet Fanny Adams – mutilated,
immortalised, profaned unthinkingly!

The murder and rape of children
seem beyond words, understanding, iniquity
– and another's lack of love or the means to love
is out of our grasp, lost beyond finding.

Parting the Ways

Earthmovers roared, made a whirling progress
six days a week: a four-lane highway
to bypass our provincial town. Gone were
Traveller's Joy, Heartsease, Love-in-Idleness.
Our wood and its narrow roadway - a lovers'
thoroughfare - severed. Only clay was left
from world's edge to world's end: a no-man's-land,
a dried-up riverbed. One Sunday,
our daughter crossed the silent excavation
and, from the opposite bank, called out:
'It's just like the Red Sea!' And she waved.
We acknowledged the future lovingly.

The Outing

Each Armistice Day, she remembered it.
A walk along the riverbank. Her teacher took them –
one Saturday when the hawthorn was out
and the river slow after weeks of sun –
her and three of the other older girls.
Miss Davies' young man came too –
in his uniform, on leave from the front.

When they all rested in the shade of a willow,
he unwrapped a large bar of chocolate
slowly, looking away, or pretending to,
across the river. Suddenly he turned.
'Voila!' he said, holding it out to them.
'Pour vous. From plucky little Belgium.'

Miss Davies and her young man went and sat
at the river's edge, their heads almost touching.
Two of her friends began whispering – another
pursed her lips and kissed the air. The others giggled.
She lay back – and squinted at the sun through the branches.
'Look', said one of the girls. The soldier was pretending
to dip the toe of his boot in the water.
Miss Davies laughed.

On the way back, 'Listen', he said, and they stopped.
On the dappled path, blocking their way,
a song thrush was striking a snail on a stone
again and again and again.

Trigger at The Adelphi, Liverpool, March, 1954

For Alex Cox

This is the year Dien Bien Phu falls,
Algeria rises, segregation is
ruled illegal in the USA,
the first kidney is transplanted and UK
wartime food rationing finally ends.

Lime Street was filled with thousands of boys and girls,
gathered to greet the singing, celluloid,
Born Again cowpoke, Roy Rogers (erstwhile
Leonard Slye), and his entourage – combining
a promo tour with a Billy Graham
crusade. The youngsters, pinched with cold on that
blitzed and windy street, clutched their copies
of the Roy Rogers Cowboy Annual.
Those with seafaring dads – and there were ships
filling the Mersey then and its docks –
had something from the Sears catalogue
of Roy Rogers' Gifts: boots, guitar, holster,
ersatz buckskin fringed shirt. (Roy and his wife, Dale,

had been mobbed in London, fringes ripped from
the genuine article). But Roy and Dale
were in bed with 'flu in their Adelphi suite –
so Trigger trotted the route alone,
climbed the hotel steps, made his mark at
reception, entered the residents' lounge,
visited his master's bedroom and appeared
at a first floor window for a photo op.

But was it Trigger or, his double,
Little Trigger? And which rears on its hind legs
stuffed in the Roy Rogers' Museum,
Branson, Missouri, the 'Show Me' state?
Or is either or both with Roy and Dale –
and Bullet, the dog, of course – alive, well and
moseying along on the moon's dark side?

While You Were Sleeping

You were here last year in your mother's womb
at this cottage high above the straits.
Now you grab for buttercups, daisies, clover,
self-heal – and edge toward sleep in the stillness
under the parasol. Ringlet butterflies
flit across the grass. Blackbirds forage
among the mulch of last autumn's leaves
at the margin where garden and woodlands merge.
A pheasant rattles somewhere out of sight.
Watching over you is a privilege.

Some time since last year, a sheep, lost in the woods,
died at the lawn's edge. An elderberry
sapling is growing through the skull. The trees –
ash, oak, beech – are loud with hidden insects.
Nearby, a pair of buzzards is breeding.
They soar above us suddenly, calling:
pee-yah, pee-yah – hover, then bank away
over the tree line. And just as suddenly
the air is replete with other birds – swifts,
swallows, house martins, a jay, a herring gull.

On the mainland, roiling clouds envelop
Moel Wnion and the Carnedd range beyond,
their iron age settlements and the sheep runs,
and thick rain, all shades of grey from pencil
to gun metal, fills Bethesda's slate quarries.
A military jet rip-roars the length
of the straits, simulating the Persian Gulf,
and a small factory ship thrums steadily,
hoovering mussels from their beds for Spain.
It's a chancy universe, little one!
But here the sun still shines. You are waking.

A Bit of a Shambles

Before Churchill took the railings, evacuees
from Liverpool were lined up by the park
one September Sunday afternoon.
Local residents queued to take their pick.
Innocent days! My widowed Granny
and two spinster aunties – ex-Scousers
(though Sefton Park not Scottie Road),
the sisters Great War collateral damage –
lined up to do their duty. They couldn't cope.
The one they chose used the 'f word'
and wet the bed. They gave her back
– and mentioned her, and what she might
have been, until they died.

A Terrible Place

Posing for the camera's long exposure,
his right foot firmly on the sledge, in bone
numbing, heart contracting temperatures,
was perhaps what brought that look into Scott's eyes.
And the eyes always have it: his say,
'I do not want to be here'. Maybe that's
twenty-twenty hindsight since we know
how it ends, with all the heroes dead.

Once this seemed to me a simple tale
of jingoism, derring do, class and
sacrifice, a prequel to The Somme.
Now, it's all about him. That look speaks
of the loneliness of leadership,
the courage of enduring duty.
He was the last to die; his log's last entry
'For God's sake look after our people!';
the last he saw of the world the tent's
beating canvas lashed by the howling wind.

Kliptown, Soweto – April 2010

Thunder wakes me, rolling over the townships,
then the suburbs south of the city, and eastward
    over the veldt.

Heavy rain falls suddenly, bouncing off the vehicles
in the secured, hotel car park.

The Klipspruit, which flows past the vast,
abandoned gold reefs, will have risen, inundating
the shacklands, their improvised shanties,
dirt streets and hard won gardens –
and I think of the rain falling on the newly paved
Walter Sisulu (erstwhile Freedom) Square,
the other side of the railway tracks.

Standing on the footbridge yesterday,
I could hear the distant call to prayer from Lenasia
on the higher ground beyond the river.
A flock of Brown Ibis flew over –
their rasping cries, loud, unsettling.

A long, yellow commuter train left the station,
moving slowly under the bridge. After it,
two people crossed the rails from the old street market
to the 'informal settlement' – a middle aged woman
in traditional township dress and a teenage girl
pristine in her Jozi school uniform.

Thunder wakes me – a low, loud, prolonged
concatenation, explosions like blastings,
the clangour of wagons shunted,
reverberating...

'Crossing the Tracks'
I, II & III, 2010

Natural Selection

Sitting on the bench on our patio, sipping
our peppermint teas one August morning,
we saw five buzzards leisurely circling
the church spire, a quintet of raptors,
four of a kind – and a joker for crows
and jackdaws to mob. But what is the prey
in this suburb for so many to survive?

The Romans built a road from Deva
to the salt pans on the plain over this heath
and its brook and through its hollows. Heather
and gorse, under the Normans, became
a habitat for outlaws – until
the overgrown road was used for droving beasts
in their hundreds, thousands to market.
Prisoners of the '45 were tried
where the brook turns north. When the railways came,
developers built villas and terraces –
between the wars, semis. Bedsits and druggies
arrived. But we are gentrified now –
sharing with the Brown Rat our good fortune.

The first buzzard I ever saw was perched
in an oak in the Ogwen Pass. Gamekeepers'
poison, myxie rabbits and pesticides
had all but extinguished them from the lowlands.
The gamekeepers went to war, 5 per cent
of the rabbits survived, pesticides
were regulated and these predators
thrived, needing less sustenance per day
than kestrels or sparrow hawks or kites –
being ambushers and opportunists.
So, here's to the buzzards and the rats –
and us, lords of them all!

A Jar of Sticklebacks

'For a thousand years…are…as a watch
in the night.' Psalm 90, The Authorized Version.

We are looking for Roary Lion and
Twit Whu Owl, my granddaughter and I –
sitting companionably side by side
on the sofa, she not yet one, me close
to the 'days of my years', as the psalmist says –
lifting the flaps on each of the pages
to find the beasts and release the sounds, she
concentrating like a biblical scholar
until, as a devil or an angel,
not unreasonably, boredom arrives.
She turns, climbs up her Grandpa, first tries to
remove his beard tuft by tuft, and then does
the old Milton Berle gag with his glasses
and laughs – and suddenly I remember
my grandpa, at my age now, his only
son recently dead, his two brothers,
Red Army officers, killed in action,
their families massacred at Babi Yar.

One day, with my mother, I netted
three sticklebacks in a pond on the Heath.
She carried them home in a jam jar.
I took it, insisting at four I could
go alone, up the back steps of the flats
to show Grandpa. I dropped it, watched it
shatter on the concrete. He heard my wails,
picked up the frantic fish, found a new vessel.

Twelve months ago you were someone we knew
nothing about but a heartbeat. Now you are
unmistakably, uniquely you –
a chortling learner, a voracious wit.
Nevertheless, it may be some time
before you decipher these signs, even
longer before they have meaning.
So, if you do, when you do, imagine me
holding up to the light, unbroken,
a jar with all your wishes, all your hopes.

Afterword

This collection is about people: some of whom I know or have known, some of whom are living or dead, fictional or historical. They are usually depicted in their familial, political and/or social environments.

Poetry in some ways is the easiest of the arts. It is solitary and comparatively economical in terms of time-over-task. The technology needed is minimal - just a pencil and some paper. No violins or blocks of Carrara marble.

I have always had things I want to say about love and death and human history, pictures I wanted to create, stories I wanted to tell. Making poetry has been part of my life for nearly fifty five years. It is a compulsion. I cannot imagine ever saying to myself, I shall write no more poems.

The poets who have influenced me are those the music of whose poetry, its rhythms and syntax, has stayed with me as much as, in some cases more than, their subject matter. They have all written poems that I return to again and again, as touchstones and for inspiration and solace.

They include, in alphabetical order:

W.H. Auden; Robert Browning; e.e. cummings; Emily Dickinson; Robert Frost; Seamus Heaney; Ted Hughes; Philip Larkin; Robert Lowell; John Milton; Wilfred Owen; Sylvia Plath; Peter Porter; William Shakespeare; W.D. Snodgrass; Alfred Tennyson; W.B. Yeats.

The lines of the poems in the collection do not begin with a capital letter unless the line is the start of a sentence. I was prompted to depart from that long tradition after reading the work of the Black Mountain Poets. Like them, I believe the lines flow more effectively.

For the same reason, there are no rhyming words at the end of lines. The only rhymes are what is known as internal and are usually half rhymes, as in these four lines from **Under November Skies:**

Rain clouds are blackening the mountains
to the west but northwards, beyond bracken
and gorse that stretches seemingly to land's edge,
through a gap in the hills, we can see the sea…

Some of the poems, like **Kliptown, Soweto, April 2010,** are in free verse, but most average ten syllables per line. The basic rhythm of those poems is what is known as iambic pentameter – ten syllables per line, in pairs of syllables, unstressed followed by stressed, as in the last line of the eponymous poem, A Jar of Sticklebacks – 'a jar with all your wishes, all your hopes'. But that is only the underlying beat and one from which I freely depart to create a range of emotions, images, thoughts and tones.

David Selzer, October 2011

Acknowledgements
At Mycenae 1984 and A Short History were first published in **The Times Literary Supplement** and **Life Lines** (University of Chester, 2005) respectively and subsequently published on www.davidselzer. com launched in 2009. Other poems in this collection previously published on the same website include: A Bit of a Shambles, Accidents, Chuzpah, Far Above Rubies, George Gershwin at Chirk Castle, Lost, Parting The Ways, Portrait of the Artist, Looking for Puffins: South Stack Revisited – A Poem for our Daughter, The Fall of Europe, The Outing, Trigger at The Adelphi Hotel, Liverpool, March 1954, While You Were Sleeping.

About the Author

David Selzer was born in London in 1942 but has lived in Chester for most of his life. He began writing poems when he was 14. His collection, 'Elsewhere', edited by Harry Chambers and published by E.J. Morten in 1973, was one of the first in the Peterloo Poets Series. He is an Eric Gregory Award and Felicia Hemans Prize winner.

After some thirty years in education, as a teacher and adviser, mostly for Cheshire County Council, David Selzer has since 2001 written four screenplays and two stage plays. One of the latter, 'Hear The Drums', earned him a prize in the 2009 Sussex Playwrights Club full length play competition. He has also begun work on two novellas and continues to write poems, which he has published on his website, www.davidselzer.com, since its launch in 2009.

About the Photographer

Sylvia Selzer LRPS is photographer in residence at Action Transport Theatre, a company specialising in work for, with and by young people. Her 'Crossing the Tracks' photographs were taken on a recent visit to Soweto, where the organisation was working with local emerging talent.

Featured in **A Jar of Sticklebacks**:
'South Stack Ynys Môn', 2009 – **Looking for Puffins: South Stack Revisited – A Poem for our Daughter**
'Window, Ancestors' House – Kwazulu-Natal', 2006 –
The Valley of the Amarici, Kwazulu-Natal, April 2006
'Crossing the Tracks' I, II & III, 2010 – **Kliptown, Soweto, 2010**
Portrait of David Selzer

About Armadillo Central:

Armadillo Central is an independent London-based publisher of new fiction, poetry and non-fiction, showcasing the best writing alongside original and limited edition art and photography, all available worldwide.

www.armadillocentral.com

www.ingramcontent.com/pod-product-compliance
Lightning Source LLC
Chambersburg PA
CBHW020953030426
42339CB00004B/73